Learning to Love a River

April 22, 2018

Learning to love a river

For Barb
with all
my best.

MICHAEL MINOR

Mik Minor

Clarise Foster, Editor

Signature
EDITIONS

Cover design by Doowah Design.
Cover photo: "Stationnement/Parking Lot" by Phil Grondin.
Photo of Michael Minor by Steph Minor.

This book was printed on Ancient Forest Friendly paper.
Printed and bound in Canada by Marquis Book Printing Inc.

We acknowledge the support of The Canada Council for the Arts and the Manitoba Arts Council for our publishing program.

Library and Archives Canada Cataloguing in Publication

Minor, Michael, author
        Learning to love a river / Michael Minor.

Poems.
ISBN 978-1-77324-027-5 (softcover)

        I. Title.

PS8626.I59L43 2018   C811'.6   C2018-901291-9

Signature Editions
P.O. Box 206, RPO Corydon, Winnipeg, Manitoba, R3M 3S7
www.signature-editions.com

for Thunder Bay
the people
the place

Learning to Love a River

In Place

Thunder Bay by Air

We burn through
a different layer of the atmosphere.
The motif of
white cloud over blue lake
finally ends.

The patchwork brown gray white
of early spring city
farmland
creeps up
to surprise us
after so much sameness
lake tree rock.

I am traveling between
more likely homes of Ottawa
and Winnipeg,
but Thunder Bay is now
thirty-eight thousand feet below.

Mission Island clearly defined
by the Kaministiqua.
All the roads
bridges, tracks
complete and intact
but small, compact.
No straight line prairie grids.
No Ottawa suburb pools.
A city formed by tactic
opportunity.

It crouches
animal-like
spoons the shore of Superior
as if trying to hide
from me.

Outside

White Otter Lake Revisited

I

Two days of dipping paddles
      chasing sun's reflection on clean brown water.
Blueberries fatten in late summer's sun;
      Canadian Shield returning light's energy.

Lining the canoes over shallow creeks
      scrapes of aluminum left flashing on the rocks.

We are not the first people to come this way
      our aluminum joins curls of red and green polymer from earlier canoes.
The final portage beside the small falls
      dense pitch-encrusted spruce.

Finally, the lake with sun-blue water and white-gold sand.
      Cliffs welcome a *swimmer's moment.*
      Remaining forest grime diffuses through cool water.

II

We're not here for
White Otter castle
　　　whispered rumours
　　　of a dead pioneer
　　　squaring the white pine himself
　　　with an axe for
　　　his truant mail-order bride.
　　　Paddled a week
　　　to bring in windows from Ignace.

Nor the POW camp
　　　abandoned since world war II
　　　too remote
　　　to escape.

But the beach.

Standing in the last daylight
looking clear across
to the other shore
eyes pan blue water
settle on the skyline of white pines
the island across from our campsite.

This beach, too,
encircled by pines.
I sprint beside them
barefoot in night-cool sand.
Running courses
through my body.

When sand gives way to rock
I am only breath and thirst
the lake swallows me.

Just my head above the water
swimming like a moose.
As my head goes under
I open my mouth to drink
synchronize
heartbeat,
sounding.

Books and Islands

People have probably been writing books in North America since at least 2000 B.C. or painting islands. You could think of the lakes as libraries.

—Louise Erdrich

lie back in the stern of a canoe
place a pack behind you for added comfort
if you are careful your partner won't even notice
you lily dipping

on Lake of the Woods
you glide under the cool cliffs
see water jigging
refracted light on the granite overhang
see *atisikan* images
speaking through millennia:
manoominikeshii the rice spirit
mikinaak the turtle at the bottom of it all
binessi the thunder bird
whose voice still echoes off of these cliffs.

If islands are books
the lakes libraries
How should I read these?

Northern Lights Lake

We buried Karl
in the coarse gold sand
up to his neck.
Pines lined the beach,
cedars the creek.

Used a tree
to lever boulders
off a cliff to feel
the suction
of the water
in our chests
when they splashed.

Smelled
ancient life of moss
feeding
on the rocks
while we slept.

Buoy Island, Lake of the Woods

To the passengers on the airplane overhead,

You passed over our heads in stretched seconds
faint engine noise
expanding chem trail
Did you notice our faint fire glow?
Did you notice four canoes spooning on the rocks?
Could you see lakes opening up a continuum with sky?

We saw
        heard your cabin
afloat the ocean of air.
How brief and long your voyage seems,
to us of open canoes
gazing up at you,
        pressurized in your leather seats.
How will you emerge from your cocoon in Calgary or Vancouver,
while we remain
half the continent away?

Mokomon Road (1)

Slap. Happening down dirt road. Slap.
Potholes. Spruce branches smack
screech down the side of the car.

Plink pellets into pop cans. Pop
squirrel with a twenty-two.
Slit it, skin it, stew it.
If you eat it, you can kill it.

Mushrooms like Munch, but painting peckers. Like,
can I eat them, Papa?
If you name it
you own it—
eat.

Mokomon Road (2)

The creek finally meets the river
rarely used railroad tracks
running beside.

Walk either way
beside the fat
brown Kaministiqua
ten miles above Kakebeka falls.

You can hear space
using echolocation

train whistles
rifle shots.

Time measured like whisky.
How many fingers
between sun
and horizon?

First Kill

There's never a shortage of partridge
when you don't have a gun in your hands.

      A guy in cub scouts
      claimed to have decapitated a partridge
      using a thin sheet of shale
      flicked backhanded
      like a skipping stone.

      Hiking around the Sleeping Giant
      the partridge killer yelled
      "Chicken!"
      every time a partridge appeared.
      As if it could tell we didn't have a gun, no shale.

But there's no partridge now.
Wandering up the tawny grass-covered road,
my grandpa's four ten,
in my arms.

Only as we crunch back up the gravel road in the car
does a partridge dare appear.
Shaking I load the gun, step out
pellets spray,
grazing the bird,
but still it tumbles down the bank.

When you cut open a partridge
everything is so orderly.
Two handfuls of clean pink-white meat
practically fall out of the bird.
And not a single pellet inside.

Mukwa

is Anishinaabemowin for bear
but this dog is no bear.
Built like a black coyote
tail waving proud
yes, black
but this dog is no bear.
A false name
the first in a long line
of her misfortunes.

Joe asked Jim,
my dad,
to take care of her
you know
like mafia
take care of.

The car ride out to the cabin
no speaking,
the dog beside me
on the back seat
dead dog sleeping

Doors click open and we emerge,
the heavy smell of boreal forest,
chamomile and dirt road,
echo of woodpecker construction.

Mukwa
trots down the hill
looks back at us.

My dad has the three-o-eight,
Hamm hand carved stock.
In one smooth motion he
raises the rifle to his shoulder
aims

Mukwa flinches

I build a fire while my Dad digs a grave.
We roast wieners on green poplar switches,
then head for home.

Smudge Ceremony

*How dare you assert the identity of a thing
with something else when your gaze tells you
that it is beyond all naming?*
—Tim Lilburn, *Return to the Garden*

At our first campsite
we shred our map
along with some wild sage,
sweetgrass
and cedar,
braid them together and burn it.
Waft the smoke
       with cupped hands
          over our eyes
         our ears
our whole bodies
ask for forgiveness.

The next day we paddle into a lake
we dare not name.

Skate Away On

Before the snow comes
if the temperature
drops suddenly
the lake freezes solid
and flat for farther than words let you see.
Stars tempt you
to stand with your neck craned
your skates rigid beneath you.
All molecules approach
stasis
no friction to speak of.

Such an improbable journey
the light of shrunken suns has taken
to meet you.
Alone and stilling
on what is only the biggest lake in the world
sliding over water
hulking skeletons of iron ships
sunk beneath your feet.

Bush Tea

On the side of a gravel road
two old friends build a spruce-bough fire.
Smoke plumes grey-brown thick
with steam from melted snow.

Coffee can with coat-hanger handle
propped over fire on a forked stick

William tears the corner from the teabag
and sprinkles half over the water, pockets the rest.

Jim and William sip around the loose tea and bits of bush
floating in their enameled mugs, but drink the winter silence.

Camp Sauna

Frozen for months
most camps empty
chimneys smokeless
save one
serenely piling
grey on grey.

Despite cold serenity
there is heat
inside the sauna.
Steam streams.
All backs arc
at the mineral kiss of
water on hot rocks.

On three, boys burst out
and pencil jump
into a hole in the ice
erase the hard rule
of winter.

Midnight Sauna

Once the steam
from our bodies clears,
just before we freeze,
dark and cold
remove every obstruction
to perception.

Lying on
ancient rocks
beside the lake.
Our eyes
duller points
of light
in the night sky.

Sailing Superior

Avoid Dog Island
to keep your keel.
Even on hot days
Gitche Gumee stays cold.

When still
lie with your belly on the bow
hang out over the water
it could be a trick of light
or the spiny back of a sturgeon
rippling deeper into the lake.

When rough
tie yourself down
with the sheets from the mast
and listen to the secrets
the lake howls in your ear.

Getting Out

After Stan Rogers

head down
low beams
cruise control
burnt coffee

just drive
make it to Winnipeg overnight
click west through the miles of
cruel curving roads
through the rock cut cathedrals
you know by heart

as the sun rises behind
scythe
long straight lanes
through grain, oil seeds
watch the city rise before you

Sister
Brother

Branwyn in the Blueberries

She does not care
about the black bear snuffling
in the next blueberry patch.

Placed in front
of a prolific bush
hand to mouth
hand to mouth
blue on baby
fingers and face.
Intent.

Beaver

While most sleep
it waddles out of the creek to chew.
Poplar chips cover the ground as
the animal works a compulsive, gravitational magic
much older than the houses and cement
that now threaten the creek.

Not will that works
the beavering jaws
but a force at once
less sensible and holier.
The tree inevitably drawn toward land
and across a bicycle path.
The squat brown beaver
gravitates back to the water.
With a slap of tail
it submerges
is gone.

Later
in pre-dawn dark
a cyclist is thrown
when he blindly strikes the tree.

In collision
wilderness baffles the city;
the rider
realizes his longing
for the earth beneath the asphalt.

10 Mile Road Race

After fourteen kilometres
I am lost in the wilderness
of my own body.

Shouldn't have watched
The Sound of Music last night:
"fa a long long way to run"
on repeat
repeat
repeat
pounding feet, pounding head
one – two – three – four
one – two – three – four
count to one hundred
make it up one more hill
to the next hydro pole, lamppost
then just breathing
panting, really.
There is no more rhythm
no rhyme
just pain of hamstrings seizing
blood hammering arhythmically in my ears

I walk the rest of the race
writing this poem
writing this poem in my head.

Suburban Bear

In Germany
bears skulk the edges of sleep
stand on hind legs
blend into forest edge
slink into motion
silent on four paws
track oblivious passers by
warn through Grimm fairy tales
of wilderness danger.

Driving
you pick out a bear
with early morning headlights.
Not all fur and fang
as the story says.
Still, you slow to idle.
It turns close-set eyes on you
looks away and pads
across the remaining pavement.

No storybook bear or
spectre from our colonial past.
A warning of the future

like obese kids on the news
with rickets and scurvy,
over   fed
under   nourished.

Brother bear lives at the dump
paws through dirty diapers.

Becky

ambles the aisles
of the warehouse-lit supermarket
as if she were circling a lake:
the shelves are unnatural, straight
lines of trees.

She is nonchalant,
foraging for flour and meat
maybe some
Pepsi.

As always she wears a black
Mennonite style headcovering,
long skirts
and practical black shoes
armour against
the imposed environment
of the supermarket.

She totters, smiles
as if to melt the walls
to leave us standing
in the forest.

Going Home

Sid works open the basement window
slithers in
tumbles onto an old mattress.

He is no thief,
already has more
than he can carry
lead brick liver
he is working to dissolve
with whatever
solvents he can find.

Years have passed
since he boarded here
to go to high school
while his family lived up north.
But this is still
his safe place.

With brewery breath
he goes in search of food
stale tortilla chips,
crumbs left on the counter.

As the chips
soak up the booze
he remembers
this is no longer his home
and falls asleep
head on the kitchen table.

In first light
the homeowner discovers Sid sleeping
coughs to wake him
and offers a ride to detox.

Once released
Sid will return
to his job
at the Days Inn front desk
until his next visit home.

Jacko

In the bar nearest his house
on Dawson Road he brags
his donkey is a better pet
than any dog. Jacko can sense his truck
five minutes out. He takes another pull
from his greasy mug.

Meanwhile
drunk hunters
pull up
in a four by four
shoot Jacko.
Do they think he's a moose?

He lives
although he has a hole
punched through him.

Perhaps he is Balaam's donkey
and they have beaten a voice
into him:
see the hole in his side.
And believe?

Evidence of a Tree Planter Returning

A trail of dirt leads to the door
the smell
sweat, DEET, sunscreen,
dirt, fertilizer
hint of Drakkar Noir
combine to produce
a synthetic pheromone,
tree-planter
musk.

Result of
days-long scratching
machine-like
in the dirt
"one-two-tree"
plunge into the scarified dirt
throw it in and stomp.
"Christmas Toe"
"March Toe"
names for when
he can feel
his stomping-foot
big toe again.

Hauls his bones
over what was forest,
and finally
up the stairs
towards the shower.

Glimpses of Al

Husqvarna school
of art.

Like
shaking hands
with a blond
tree.

Keeps
his keys
in the ignition:
only he
can start
the ancient
powder-blue
Dodge Ram.

William

I've known him all my life
as Cornelius,
this aging Anishinaabe
sitting across from me
on the city bus.
Winter has driven his hands
deep into his heavy, beaded mittens.
The overheated bus
draws them out again.

> I remember him in church basements.
> A serious man
> in turn taken seriously.
> He would pray in Anishinaabemowin
> for a quarter hour at a stretch
> his audience rapt,
> though few understood.

> Just a year ago he learned
> he had not been baptized Cornelius.
> With the authority of a man
> named by God
> he patiently corrects
> all who call him Cornelius:
> "my name is William."

On this hot bus he is
oblivious to my presence,
sitting sideways,
hands folded on his stomach
eyes closed.
Do those hands
that skinned unnumbered rabbits
now belong to William?

He may be praying
or simply asleep.

The Blue Spruce

stands up
for wildness
in the face of the civil
lies told by the humming wires
overhead in the back alley

It stands
a bit crooked
as houses crumble
cars rust to dust
and grows
slightly taller

Winter Runner

He moves fast
through bone cold,
is easily missed.
Chalk it up to
snow blindness
or wind-frozen
eyes.

Incessant movement
one way to stay alive
in *the lazy wind,*
too lazy to go around.

He carries this knowledge
wherever he travels
Caribbean islands
or muggy American cities in August
he can always recall
the smell
of synthetic fabric frozen
with sweat
close to his nose:
the icy collar
of his jacket.

Sleeping Giant

Like *Nanabijou*
stretched stone-cold
across the water
I sleep heavily
with water pouring
on the roof
thunder answers
lightning's call
parents murmur in the kitchen,
I know they are there
but still I am
sinking slowly into the bed.

The Berry Picker

She travels
alleyways
with a tin can around her waist
redeeming
destitute green patches
where drunks
have slept, smashed
their bottles
where neighbourhood dogs
mark their territory
        where raspberries grow.

Early on summer mornings
she heads out
by bicycle
and when the pavement stops,
by foot.
Picks what berries she finds
to eke out a batch of jam:
12 red jars cooling on the counter.

She thinks of
her children
around the Christmas morning table
with jam in their teeth.

Sees berries
when she
closes her eyes.

Cameron Street

and I'd walk in step
to my own heartbeat
when I was a paper boy,
when I was a paper boy.
                            —David Francey, "Paper Boy"

The paper boy pulls a homemade wagon
wheels from an old pram
chipboard box
loaded with papers
or flyers each Thursday.

Feels like it's
always winter.
His footprints
first in the morning snow,
framed by stubborn
wheel tracks.
His toes and fingers
stiffening with cold.
Smells of pancakes
cooking in kitchens,
sees heat and steam
rising from chimneys,
radio crackling the same
Peter Gzowski voice
that waits for him at home
as his mother
fries eggs.

As he comes to the last house
on the even side of the block
he feels alone
but brave.
Chipboarded windows,
pink insulation poking out at the corners,
and a fake brick facade.

Knows when they do not pay
he will have to call
cancel their subscription.

McIntyre River

Someone must love
the McIntyre River.

Each time I cross
one of four bridges,
the usual brown water
trash floating
ducks
a rusted cart imitating a shipwreck
and greying couple too stubborn
to admit their canoeing days are done

Trees still grow
in profusion on your banks
partly obscure the garbage.
They drink deeply
of your stinking slurry.

We dared Karl
to swim across
he caught nothing worse
than pinkeye.
No, not toxic after all.

This is for all the rivers
in all the cites
that incredibly
are not toxic
but deadly.

For you are not
Lake Superior,
you've given up
your dead.

I am still trying to love you;
someone must love you.

Redneck

The Chevy Silverado
has a bumper sticker
"I'd rather be *walking*
on the side of the road with a Chevy
steering wheel in my hand, than
driving a Ford."
You can buy them
in rural gas stations
usually next to the one with
the mischievous cartoon Calvin
pissing on Chevy,
Ford, or GMC logos,
often next to the truck nuts
and the literal-minded bumper declaration
"this truck's got balls!"

The red Silverado
is only two years old
but he wants a new one
wants deer meat out of season.

Driving East on 11-17
quiet save the hum
of knobby off-road tires on pavement
the rumble of the engine.
Just before Dorion his headlights
bounce off the deer's
green eyes.

He swerves to hit it.

Duck

I wanted to see through… Big Heavens
—Louise Halfe, *The Crooked Good*

Joe stands in the small motorboat
draws his slingshot in a straight line
releases the glass marble.
It *sshwnks* into the water
just past the mallard's emerald head.

At ten years old, I'm drawn to slingshots
not fishing. My rod rests on the gunwales.
Joe feeds another marble into the leather pouch
draws, releases, connects.
With the crack of marble on bird-bone
the neck crumbles
a dropped marionette.

Joe eases the boat beside the still-floating duck
cradles the glistening body in both hands.
Lifting it out of water, he closes his eyes
as water droplets from feathers rejoin the lake.

The mallard rests at the bottom of the boat.
On the way back to our campsite,
I glance furtively into the mallard's lifeless eye
and Joe's, his *Big Heavens.*

In Place

In a Name

The ballot said:
Lakehead
The Lakehead
Thunder Bay

Little debate about
amalgamation itself,
but full-on fights
about "the."
They both lost
split the vote.
And so we became Thunder Bay
from the French:
Baie du Tonnerre
from Anishinaabemowin
animikii, thunderbird.

Still some
who sulk
walk dour-faced
in Intercity Mall
muttering *The* Lakehead.

Mission Island

Some call it home:
        coal power plant
        yacht club
        natural reserve
        scrap metal
        deer who have forgotten
                        what they are
        you, the runner

cross the bridge enter the jumble
of wild and tame. Deer eat
apples from green garbage bags, grow
fat on misguided charity, walk
too often on the road, fodder
for ravenous cars.

Catch a deer looking
askance into the bush
or at a passing train. The animal
smell of your sweat
may remind it of the loaded springs in its legs.
It may deke-dance with you awhile. Then forget
join the herd
resume the sedentary way
of a deer in the city.

Show

a cross-country skier.
She breaks a path
down our sleeping
residential street
after four feet of snow.
The only one moving
this morning of a snow day:
red lycra slips through
the still whiteness.

How pigeons
with pearl-smooth breast feathers
fat and beautiful cooing
under the CP rail bridge
make me duck
imagine them shitting on me
each time I pass under.

and Tell

on this very spot
fur traders with too tall guns
took bales of beaver pelt
in exchange for whisky.

By the time the trapper left
a winter's work:
a whisky reduction
of hangover
and debt.
There was nothing left to show.

Fort William

Even before
modern waterways
you could
get a York boat to the mouth
of the Kaministiqua
with horses
beautiful black
hairy-hoofed animals.
Hauling ploughs
through uncut soil,
pulling spruce and birch stumps.
There were oxen,
an armory,
cooper, blacksmith.
One might imagine
Anishinaabeg looking in amazement
as horse-powered plows
sparked against rocks.

But no white man would be here without
bark canoes
negotiating rivers
to the sea on either side.
Thousands of pounds — men,
fur, supplies —
ferried to the middle
of Thompson's map,
and further.

McKenzie feverishly drove
his crew through the continent.
Willed water
to change course
lead him to his white whale,
the Pacific.
I heard they ate their
moccasins on that trip.

Now, university students
dressed as North West Co. partners
        period wool jackets
        beaver felt top hats
sneak into the modern kitchen
and place their thick coats
in the freezer.

In the dog days of summer
students with thick black coats,
mysteriously cool,
among unsuspecting
sweating American tourists.

Their Garden

When the grown children ask them
about moving out
they begin to talk
about their garden.

If they left,
who would note the shifts in weather?
Answer for what grows over a short dry summer?
The unexpectedly frostless September?

If they left,
who would find rusted things half buried, forgotten?
Harvest unnamed plants that grow without planting?

Over time, emphasis
slowly changed
from family-feeding beets
to lavender and basil.

As mother washes the basil
she reads
When I am Old I Will Wear Purple
as if to explain new clothes
or her love of lavender
without saying words.

She allows mint its empire
beside the house.
That single bean
sprouted for Ms. Redfern's
grade four class
now a dynasty.

Father waters the elephantine pink peonies
and though he checks the zucchini daily,
some elude and
swell to civic monuments
beneath broad shady leaves.

Only two left
to eat this excess.

They watch their garden grow
slow, gather small
comfort in roots
that are not legs running
or wheels rolling away.
Roots that reach gradually
break up hard pieces
in the loam.

Tikinaagen

The cradle board
on top of the piano
does not belong.

I don't know
why Magnus James made one
for a white family.
Its form reflects the contradiction
the beautiful applique on moosehide
with unfortunate paint colours of the 1970s.

It sat on the piano
evoking incongruous safety
the support of something
sturdy against my back.
Imagine myself an infant
cocooned, looking out the living room window,
my mother watering plants.

Farmer's Market

People have put down roots,
despite bedrock, the Canadian Shield
and long winters,
this is land to pull strength from.

Tomatoes slow and steady
in September:
small but fierce
yellows, reds, and purples.

And root vegetables
like bearded men
in Carhartt jackets
rubbing calloused hands against the cold.

We bought a basket of beans
crisp in the fall air.

Apples: compact, tart
pink and yellow
under healthy
white powder
proof of waxless origin.

The year-long scent of spruce,
Vicks strong in our nostrils,
cuts across the palate
and draws strength from black muskeg
into our bones.

Adanac Hotel

No VLTs since the Casino came,
but the same crowd
wearing flannel
red and black
check.
Elbows on the bar.

Brown bottles
for self-defense.
You're finished in a fight
if all you've got
is a plastic Coors Light cup.

No poetic oddity:
a water colour
of a tulip behind the bar
Bishop's *doily*
Purdy's *yellow flowers*.
It's all piss,
running down legs
out of the washrooms
into Simpson Street.

Spoons

As he stirs his coffee
he tells of plans to bring cast-off
x-ray machines, scanners, hospital beds
to grateful Caribbean islands.

Meanwhile on Simpson Street
a woman stands
on the corner.

The game is called spoons
when the white boys from the university
drive around with teaspoons
in their drink holders just in case
but in a pinch, they'll use anything at hand:
      water bottles
      fast-food leftovers

    trailer hitches

You are supposed to hit her
but if you miss, you have to get out
retrieve your spoon.

They slow as they approach
roll down the rear tinted window.
The teaspoon hits her leg.
Laughter muffled
by tires starting on snow as they escape.

But he has seen none of this.
With palm trees on repeat,
he stirs his coffee.

Morels

Had he used
the pockets of his grey coat
instead of the bag he brought
to clean up after the dog?

"Morels," he said
anticipating our disgust.
Alien foodstuffs
hatched overnight
amidst crumbling cinder blocks,
broken glass, and unidentified
detritus of the back alley.

We mix them into a pot
of Kraft Dinner,
will them to be
energized,
to st-r-r-e-e-e-tch
come alive
to hear them tell in croaking voices
the secrets of their sub(extra)terranean travels.

Scars

How hands
carry the weight
the booger welded
seams of place.
Forcing open
a container from the freezer
takes a divot
off the back of
my left
thumb.

Knees tell
the palimpsest tales of
sliding in playground gravel
wobbling off bicycles
astroturf and wrestling mats.

How else can home
unzip us,
slip beneath skin,
write itself
on our bodies?

Simonite's Grocery

A penny *was* a candy.
A dollar *was* a bagful,
no counting.

Legs couldn't
keep up
with desire
en route
to place
a sweaty dollar on the counter

and walk slowly home,
sucking on sour keys
counting each crack avoided
in the sidewalk.

Brodie Street Library

Carnegie's
shame money
made it here too.
As with a time capsule
the creators could not know
what would push up around
this unlikely temple.

Ghosts of civic pride
an all but empty mall
abandoned movie theatres
still haunt
what was once
downtown Fort William.
The deferred dreams of a city
still palpable
in the stooped streetwalkers
who search for shelter
from the sagging sky.

Each building presents
an alternate reality.
Facades — St. Andrew's red brick wall
painted to imitate stone
new City Hall
same as the old city hall
but glassier, a glorified bus stop
Carnegie's columns still stand
despite the newly "accessible" entrance
all counter balanced by
the only truly new one
the court house.

Buildings at corners
brace the tensions of then and now
propose no new solutions
to the "Indian problem."
Though mostly stagnant, industry
still pumps its pulp mill reek
in the distance.

o

From my seat
on a chunky wooden chair
I squint to make out
Brodie Street below.

How then am I so different
from the disheveled man sleep-thawing
at the table next to me?
The same stained-glass
faces of long-dead white men
look over both our shoulders.

As an exercise in empathy
I put the book down
to see if I too will sleep.
Awake surprised
to see my neighbour gone.
and a librarian
telling me
I can't sleep here.

Kamview

On the coldest nights
embrace the speed of
hard-packed snow
beneath your skis.
Everything is
silent
save the swish
of a faster skier
sliding past.
Your eyes slow
to catch up
in the next pool
of yellow light.

Your car is the last
in the parking lot.

You wonder
if the doors
are frozen shut.

Smelting

Even in the city
creeks
flash silver
by flashlight.
In the middle of the night,
smelt are running.

We dip nets,
buckets, pots and pans
empty the slippery catch
into coolers.

Tomorrow
we will sleep in.
And then in alien daylight
retrieve our bounty from
warm car trunks.
Snip heads off with scissors.

Summer silver
to feed us through winter.

March Break

We break a path
through slush,
a soaker every step.
Crystals of ice
stuck to wool socks.

Find ourselves
in present tense.
The city streets
are clear
but the Sleeping Giant
still clings to his white
blanket.

Eighteen kilometres later,
we split open soggy boots peel off socks
and dry our pulpy white feet.

The lake dares us
to enter
and drink.

We wade out until ache
gives way to burning
then numbness
drink gulping mouthfuls
straight from this fresh,
ice-water ocean.

Run

to prove
that rocks and trees and water
will not swallow you
work out how to carve
shelter from rocks and trees
to make clothes
out of animal skins

to disappear the city
just make it up one more hill
and into
the centre
of what came before.

An Insider's Guide to Thunder Bay

1 Hoito

A reminder of our lumberjack days
Finnish pancakes, 1960s cafeteria decor
large bronze scale to greet your arrival.

this is how you do it:
wait
weigh-in
order
wait
drink
eat
pay
weigh-out

lumberjacks are very hungry
don't talk much

2 Marina Park

You don't have to cut
the earth open here
to do an autopsy.
The shipping industry
died of starvation.
Along the shore
grain elevators
decay in all directions.

"We've got a giant heart"
(goes the song from the nineties)
and we wear it on our sleeves,
make only feeble attempts to hide it
from the medical examiners
with condos and festivals.

Still, you should
take a stroll in Marina Park.
Go on a Wednesday.
Watch the yacht races.
Buy an ice cream
as you wait for the elevator skeletons
to waste into the lake.

3 Mount McKay

"If you miss Mount McKay
you miss Thunder Bay"
says the requisite sign
featuring a redskin wearing feathers.
The racism
doesn't make the statement false.

First take
the Fort William First Nation road
pay the toll.
Park and walk
through muskeg,
poplar leaf-lined puddles.

Clamber over rocks,
line yourself up granite boulders
left after glaciers
chopped the top of the mountain.

With the blueberry bushes
at your feet, find the city

a footnote
of forest and lake.

4 Sleeping Giant

A matter of perspective
trace head torso
step by step (ooo baby)
stop for tea
at T harbour
scramble over his shale feet

or pick a hill in Port Arthur
and take him in
with your eyes
all at once.

Hard Times in the Neighbourhood

Each morning our neighbours would fill
a shopping cart
with empties,
rattle down the alley
to the Beer Store
come back stocked
to sell to teenagers
that night.

But, the new drug dealers offer
fewer stabbings
fewer parties.
They have a family
to provide for
after all.

Rollie moved in
across the alley.
Everyone thought he would
go under in a year or two.
I can still smell his cigars
even though he never sold that many.
Used paperbacks
in a rack by his register
for a quarter a piece.

Got a dive shop
attached to Rollie's
for all those divers
going out to Silver Islet Mine.
They dug too deep out there,
flooded the place.

And the stout Italian man
with his wide suspenders,
spotless Chevy truck with topper
garden in the porch.

East End Video has had a sign up for years
    "Closed for renovations *may* reopen August 1st"

Marg's Laundromat
Superior Bowladrome
Five Star Bakery
McIntyre River
Empty lots, Empty schools
Norm's Yachts (we shrink-wrap boats!)
Simpler Times Cremation
churches, parks
The weed-selling pizza joint that reopens under new ownership every year or two.

The guy fixing his truck
up on cinder blocks
in the front yard
across the street
has only managed
to get the radio working
"it's a great
day to be alive."

Graveside

The March sky is grey
poker-faced. The engine
of a digger burps,
scooping out another grave. We
can't get it right. We
flail, failing
to honour them.

Flowers are a poignant wink
their blossoms dead
frozen solid in seconds.

Trinkets left
rusted by the passing winter.
The decay and dying of these knickknacks
fitting perhaps,
but futile.

We stand on brown grass
slip on dirty ice.
Reduced to less than language,
we sniff into our rumpled tissues.

Give me a stone
cold without obvious
life or death.
Its opacity
makes no promises
casting the same shadow
for centuries.

Maclean's Survey

The results are in
bottom of the list
of "livable" cities in Canada,
again.
Numbers crunched include
income, unemployment
violent crime
non-violent crime
access to
        education
        employment
        public transit
        medical care
        Toronto
population density
distance between downtown cores
(dying now that the city is amalgamated)
per capita numbers for
        drunken street fights (still the champs)
        Walmarts
        coffee shops
        murders
        hockey rinks and players in the NHL
        alcohol consumption (barely lost to St. John's)

But there is no mention of
Victor Wong's patent leather boots.
This second violinist in the TBSO
who has to carry a shoehorn
everywhere he goes.

Nor the James Whalen,
a converted tugboat
freshly painted, moored
in a murmuring heart of the city.
The winter and summer
soundtrack
of Simpson Street.

They did see a drunk guy
sleeping on a bench
took his photo for the article.

But not it seems the sun
I see rising
through white chimney smoke
out my living room window.

I doubt they've smelled
apple blossoms
on Victoria Avenue
Lilacs on Wiley
Cedar in Dease Park
or Sunlight dish detergent
      from that time someone emptied ten bottles
      into the Paterson Park fountain
      and the foam spilled out onto May Street.

Did they climb the turtle
in Vickers park?
Go swimming with
tight-lipped Finns
at the Cascades?

They mustn't have looked out
from the highway
heading East
to find a lake
as big as an ocean.

Is the view from Hillcrest park
a ten?
Does it matter
If a laker's docking in the harbour
or the petunias at your feet are in full bloom?

What are snow days worth?
When you can
jump off your roof
and disappear (poof)
in a wink of whiteness?

When
thunderstorms
shake rock foundations
fill storm sewers
leave double rainbows?

When the falls
swollen and cascade
copper
dares you to race
to the lake?

These scenes
these senses,
have escaped them.

But they overwhelm us
like a cross-country skier
overtaking in the night.

Notes

White Otter Lake Revisited
Located between the Northwestern Ontario towns of Atikokan and Ignace, White Otter Lake is only accessible by air or by portage in the summer. It is best known as the site of White Otter Castle, which is a three story log structure built by Jimmy McQuat in the early 1900s. Legend would have it that his motivation for building the impressive "castle" was heartbreak, after his plans to marry Jane Gibson fell through. His body was discovered in 1919. He had apparently drowned while fishing. There are also the remains of a prisoner-of-war camp that was used to house German prisoners in World War II.

"The Swimmer's Moment" is a poem by Margaret Avison.

Books and Islands
Both the title and the spelling of the anishinaabemowin (Ojibwe language) in this poem are drawn from Louise Erdrich's book of travel writing *Books and Islands in Ojibwe Country*, which is primarily set on Lake of the Woods. The final quotation is in reference Helen Hoy's book on Indigenous literature, *How Should I Read These?*

Mukwa
Anishinaabemowin does not have a standardized spelling or even a standardized set of characters for writing the language. It has been written in many different ways. If I am referencing a specific work where spellings are provided, I adopt those spellings. In the case of Mukwa, the actual name of the dog featured in this poem, there is no written text that I am referring to, so I've chosen a spelling that approximates the pronunciation.

Sailing Superior
Gitche Gumee is not a particularly good indication of the pronunciation of this Anishinaabemowin name for Lake Superior, but it is the spelling used in the lyrics of Gordon Lightfoot's folk ballad "The Wreck of the Edmund Fitzgerald."

Getting Out
This poem is in reference to Stan Rogers' song "Northwest Passage."

Fast Runner
As many dads from cold climates will be proud to inform you, a lazy wind is one that cuts right through you, rather than going around.

Sleeping Giant
Nanabijou is one name in Anishinaabemowin for the famous rock formation, and the being that is still sleeping there, commonly referred to as the Sleeping Giant.

McIntyre River
The final lines of this poem once again reference Gordon Lightfoot's song "The Wreck of the Edmund Fitzgerald." According to this song, and popular histories, those who drown in Lake Superior are not found. Between 2001 and 2017, nine Indigenous youth from Northern communities, seven of whom were attending Dennis Franklin Cromarty High-School, have died in tragic and suspicious circumstances that were not fully investigated. Several of these youth were discovered in the McIntyre River or the floodway that has the same source. Tanya Talaga's book *Seven Fallen Feathers* tells their stories.

Duck
I owe "Big Heavens" to Louise Halfe's use of the term as a translation from the Cree word for eyes. This term appears in both *The Crooked Good* and *Blue Marrow* in the Cree forms *miskîsik* and *miskîsikwa*.

In a Name
Thunder Bay is the result of the amalgamation of Fort William and Port Arthur, which occurred in 1970. By far the most popular choice for renaming the new city was some variation on Lakehead, but because The Lakehead and Lakehead were each distinct choices, they split the vote. As a result, Thunder Bay was chosen. According to oral histories, this name has its roots in Anishinaabe (Ojibwe) teachings about the thunder bird.

Fort William
Anishinaabeg is what the Indigenous people who live in what is now called Northwestern Ontario call themselves. They have lived in this region for millennia and are a large group stretching into parts of what is now the United States and Manitoba. This group is also referred to as Chippewa, Ojibwe, Ojibwa, or Ojibway.

Adanac Hotel
Here I reference Elizabeth Bishop's poem "Filling Station" and Al Purdy's "At the Quinte Hotel."

Spoons
In January of 2017, Barbara Kentner was walking down a street in Thunder Bay when Brayden Bushby threw a trailer hitch from a moving vehicle and hit her. After a prolonged stay in hospital, she died in July from the injuries received. As of 2018, Bushby has been charged with second degree murder.

Scars
I dedicate this poem to anyone who already knows that a booger weld is not as disgusting as it sounds.

Brodie Street Library
Italics indicate another line from Stan Rogers' song "Northwest Passage."

Acknowledgements

Like many first collections, this one has come into being over several years and with the help of many remarkable people. First and foremost, I thank my parents and family, who are all featured in some way in these poems. You have heard many versions of these poems over the years; thanks for your patience and generosity as I've fictionalized our lives. Similarly, I'm grateful to the community of Thunder Bay for providing such a rich and complicated place to grow up in and to write about.

I am very fortunate to have had several poets that I deeply admire play a role in the development of this collection. Don McKay was the first reader for a few of the poems in "Outside." The ideas he presented in a course on wilderness writing that I took at Memorial University of Newfoundland have permeated this whole collection. I also owe a debt of gratitude to Méira Cook for the patient and careful editorial work done through the Manitoba Writers Guild's Sheldon Oberman Mentorship program. Many of these poems reached maturity under her watch. Thanks to everyone at Signature Editions, especially Garry Thomas Morse for the title. Clarise Foster, thank you so much for guiding this manuscript into its final form.

Some of these poems appeared in *Contemporary Verse 2*. Earlier forms of "Smudge Ceremony" and "Mukwa" also appeared in *The Antigonish Review*.

Despite my best attempts to make home in the places I've lived, I cannot escape the fact that I have been a guest. I am a descendant of my grandfather who came from Germany, and great-grandparents who came from Scotland, Ireland, Sweden, and Norway. I'm trying to be a better guest on the Indigenous land where I was born and that I currently live on.

My love to Steph, my partner in all things, and to our children.

About the Author

Originally from Thunder Bay, Ontario, Michael Minor is a settler scholar teaching and studying decolonization through Indigenous literature. He teaches academic writing at the University of Manitoba in the Inner City Social Work Program and graduated with a PhD in English Literature from the University of Manitoba in 2016. Before his time at the U of M, he completed an undergraduate degree at Trent University in Peterborough, Ontario and a Master of Arts at Memorial University of Newfoundland in St. John's. In addition to teaching and academic writing, he writes reviews for *CV2* and the *Winnipeg Review*. Some of his poetry has been previously published in the *Antigonish Review* and *CV2*. *Learning to Love a River* is his first book of poetry. He was once a runner, and has good intentions of putting in enough long runs to claim that title once again. He is also a songwriter, living in Winnipeg with his partner and their children.

ECO-AUDIT
Printing this book using Rolland Enviro 100 Book
instead of virgin fibres paper saved the following resources:

Trees	Solid Waste	Water	Air Emissions
2	74 kg	6,053 L	244 kg